THIRTY DAYS OF

Thanksgiving

AND

Praise

by
SUSAN SLADE
and
SUSIE HALE

Wyatt House Publishing
Mobile, Alabama

Wyatt House books may be ordered through booksellers or by contacting:

WYATT HOUSE PUBLISHING
399 Lakeview Dr. W.
Mobile, Alabama 36695
www.wyattpublishing.com

Because of the dynamic nature of the Internet, any web address or links contained in this book may have changed since publication and may no longer be valid.

Cover design by: Mark Wyatt
Interior design by: Mark Wyatt
ISBN 13:978-1-954798-17-5

This book is also available at amazon.com, barnesandnoble. com, and other online retailers.

Printed in the United States of America

ACKNOWLEDGEMENTS

First and foremost, we thank our Lord and Savior Jesus Christ for sustaining both of us through physical trials while completing this book project. "God chose us to be His precious jewels. We overcome life's challenges through the grace of God in order to radiate the glory of God."

Susan thanks Brother T.D. Hall who made the Good News so simple that a precocious four or five-year-old could grasp the message and surrender her life to Jesus. Susie thanks Brother G. Ray Young who left the choir practice he was directing to walk her through the Roman Road to surrender her heart to Jesus when she was fifteen.

We thank our pastor, Ben Polson, for helping us with our website and encouraging us to publish our writing. He and our church family come alongside us in many ways.

We thank Chrissy Thorpe for writing the foreword to this book and for being our MSF (Mother-Sister-Friend) and constant prayer support.

We thank Richard Albin of *Richard Wayne Photography* for the photographs of each of us and the beautiful AI assisted picture for the front cover.

We thank Jennifer Staatz of *Maker's Haven Shop* for tailoring and even designing/engineering clothing to work with Susan's earth-suit. We are so blessed to have found a seamstress extraordinaire!

We thank our prayer partner, Missy Blanchard, our cherished, chosen sister in the faith, for consistently, fervently lifting us up to the Father concerning not only our ministry but our personal lives. Missy is an independent, licensed, and ordained minister through the *National Association of Christian Ministers*.

We thank those who literally lift Susan up to transfer her in and out of her chair: Dane and Dana Carr, Chelsea Landsee, Nick Sheperd, and Zach Sullivan. They also lift us in prayer and constantly encourage us!

We thank the Precious Jewels Ministries board members: Dane and Dana Carr, Crystal Foster, Eric Little, and Nick Miller as well as our Treasurer, Rick Ivey, for their encouragement and guidance.

We thank our Generous Gems (monthly donors) who make it possible for us to self-publish books and whose generosity enables us to continue in ministry.

SOLI DEO GLORIA!

FOREWORD
by Chrissy Thorpe

What a privilege to boost "Foreword" this book of Thankfulness written by my two precious friends, Susan and Susie. I encourage you to read it with determined energy because their devotions will not disappoint you. We can join these remarkable sisters in Christ, not in maudlin sentimentality, but in the power available to each of us through grateful interaction with the Spirit of the Risen Christ, which is the only power that can carry us through the last days we seem to be living in.

I treasure their concept of God's attribute of Omnipresence, as the "alwaysness" of God with His children. They remind us that "if you have entrusted your life to Jesus Christ and received His gift of salvation, you will never be alone again." You can "bring your needs to the Lord with THANKSGIVING, and He will give you peace" (Philippians 4:6-7). [p. 15]

Life experiences gave Susie a literal understanding of "leaning heavily on Christ the solid Rock". She reminds us of our solid foundation in the love of Christ. [p. 16] You, too, can cry out to Jesus, knowing He will hear you and help you in your darkest hour.

You will be challenged to write your own Psalm, following the template of Psalm 136. Don't think you can't do it! These ladies of God put their life experiences together and created their own Psalm. [p. 26] What will your own Psalm look like? How rich will your life become as you remind yourself daily of God's goodness toward you by recalling your own Psalm?

Being thankful towards God will fill your heart with energy. These two should know. They model what they speak. Lots of devotional books encourage Christians to spend time with God. This one will challenge you to live like a believer, by putting *your money*--literally--*where your mouth is* in order to support the works of God, as they boldly recount in their donut sacrifice devotion, "Giving from Gratitude Produces More Gratitude". [p. 29]

Oh, and don't neglect to listen to each day's musical selection. What a blessing! Some days, it takes music for the message to have time to soak in.

I am proud to be a friend of Susan and Susie and am happy to recommend their *Thirty Days of Thanksgiving Praise* as a book that will help any believer "to know the love of Christ that surpasses knowledge," that you may live like they do, "filled with all the fullness of God." (Ephesians 3:19 ESV).

Chrissy Thorpe

Chrissy Thorpe has been married to Sam, a college theology professor, for 47 years. Their blessings include four children, their spouses, and 12 grandchildren. At age 53, Chrissy was able to return to college to earn a Master's degree in Practical Theology and has since been writing and teaching. Her college research was published as a textbook, Studies in Christology and Pneumatology. She enjoys her family, making jewelry, playing the piano, swimming, writing, and talking on the phone to Susan while she does laundry and cooks. Chrissy's friendship with Susan began in 1992. Because of Susan's limited earth-suit (her term) and fertile mind, that association has caused much spiritual growth between the two of them. Susie came into Susan's life in God's perfect timing, providing her with the love and care she deserved, as well as a chance to write together fulfilling both their callings. They are God's Ladies of the Spirit! Their accomplishments under the most trying physical, emotional, and financial encumbrances are miraculous and inspiring.

DEDICATIONS

We dedicate this book to the following people for persevering, remaining thankful, and living out the command of 1 Thessalonians 5:17-18 (AMP) despite difficult circumstances: ". . . be unceasing and persistent in prayer; in every situation [no matter what the circumstances] be thankful and continually give thanks to God; for this is the will of God for you in Christ Jesus." God chose them to be His precious jewels who are overcoming life's challenges through the grace of God in order to radiate the glory of God. Because of their intimate relationships with Jesus, they continue to inspire and motivate us to be thankful no matter what!

- Sarah (Home with Jesus) and T.D. Hall
  Betsy (Home with Jesus) and Dudley Hall
- Larie and Doug (Home with Jesus) White
- Sherrice and Robert Copeland
- Ray and Carol Keller
- Helen Young (Nana) and son, Mark Young
- Martha and Jimmy Dean
- Francis Scott and family
- Harold and Linda Whitten
- Ann and Jerry Hines
- Jackie and Michael Postlethwait
- Dee White

- Jon and Martina Rutherford
- Elizabeth and Ben Polson
- Karen and Mark Patton
- Sherri and Rusty Wilson
- Cody and Linda Curry
- Sheri Biggs and her dad, John Carter
- Sharon and Bob Neely
- Caitlyn and Chase Truitt
- Barrett McKim and family
- Amy and Kevin Oates and son, Isaac
- Trafton and Patricia Kelley
- Kitty and Mike Huber
- Sandra and B.H. Tarno

PREFACE:
GETTING MORE FROM THIS BOOK

1. There are thirty days in November, so you may want to read a page each day. Or you could begin reading thirty days leading up to Thanksgiving Day. We hope you will want to remain thankful all year long!

2. We quoted each focal scripture verse but suggest that you open your Bible or your Bible App, as the case may be, and read the entire passage to understand the context. We try to give enough context to avoid confusion, but the best way to read this book is with an open Bible next to it.

3. You may also want to look up any cross references that we do not quote in full. A brief devotion does not lend itself to exploring fully every cross reference.

4. We purposely left some blank space at the end of each devotional for you to record your own notes, poems, drawings, insights, or whatever helps you focus your mind on Jesus.

5. If you have children or even if you don't, think about how you would explain the content of each devotion to a first grader, or sixth grader, or preschool child. This will not only enhance your understanding of it by forcing you to break it down into its simplest form, but you will be prepared if a child asks you a question related to the de-

votion. Children often ask unusually profound questions. For example: when asked to thank God for only one thing, a 5-yr-old said, "I thank God for God."

6. You may want to read the daily devotions with your spouse, your entire family, your roommate, or your best friend. Discussion helps us retain what we read.

7. We have included opportunities for worship experiences. If you are reading this in print format, please take a few moments to type the URLs into your browser on the computer, iPad, or phone and listen to the songs. They are included not only for your enjoyment but because they will enrich your understanding of the message.

8. You may want to set aside a "date" with the Lord. Plan a time to take this book, your Bible, and maybe a notebook to a quiet place and spend an hour alone with Jesus. It can be a beautiful outdoor setting or a quiet coffee shop, just someplace you will not be disturbed or disturb others. Read, pray, sing, worship, and most importantly listen to the Holy Spirit. You may think you don't have an extra hour, but the refreshment you gain by spending time with the Lord will invigorate you to complete your normal daily tasks.

9. We have provided an index that lists all the scripture verses quoted or referenced in book of the Bible order to enable you to find a particular devotion if you are studying or teaching on one

of those verses or passages.

10. Use this book as a springboard for practicing an "attitude of gratitude" every day. We've read it takes 21 days to form a habit. Use these 30 days to form the excellent habit of thankfulness!

TABLE OF CONTENTS

Acknowledgements   5

Foreword by Chrissy Thorpe   7

Dedications   11

Preface: Getting More from This Book   13

1 Chronicles 16:8-10

Thank God for His Mighty Deeds   21

1 Chronicles 29:12-14

Thankful to be Entrusted with God's Riches   23

Psalm 28:7

Joyful Song of Thanksgiving   25

Psalm 69:30

Magnify the Lord with Thanksgiving   27

Psalm 75:1

Lord, I Thank You   *29*

Psalm 75:1

Thank God for His Omnipresence: Always Available

                                                     31

Psalm 95:1-2

Rock Concert   33

Psalm 95:1-7
I Cannot Help but Sing   *36*

Psalm 105:1-3
Call Upon His Name with Thanksgiving   38

Psalm 107:8
Gratitude for God's Deliverance   40

Psalm 116:17
Thanksgiving for Deliverance from Death   42

Psalm 118:1
Gratitude to Our God Who is Good   45

Psalm 119:62
Midnight Thanksgiving   *48*

Psalm 136
Great Praise   50

Psalm 136:1-3
Our Great Praise   *53*

Psalm 138:1-2
Thankful with all My Heart   56

Psalm 138:3 &
Be Thankful that Peace Prevails   58

Philippians 4:6-7
2 Corinthians 9:11-12
Giving from Gratitude Produces More Gratitude   60

2 Corinthians 9:15
Gratitude for God's Greatest Gift   63

Ephesians 5:19-20
Give Thanks for Everything   66

Philippians 4:6-7
Be Thankful, Not Anxious   69

Philippians 4:6-7
Give Thanks and Leave it There   *73*

Colossians 1:9-12
Prayer of Thanks for Brand New Saints   74

Colossians 2:6-7
God's Garden of Glorious, Gorgeous Flowers:
People Overflowing with Thankfulness   77

Colossians 3:15-17
Let God's Peace Reign and be Thankful   80

Colossians 3:15-17
May Gratitude Flow   *83*

Colossians 4:2-4
Be Vigilant and Thankful   85

Colossians 4:2-4
Diligent, Vigilant Prayer with Thanksgiving   *88*

1 Thessalonians 5:16-18
Thankfulness and Joy No Matter What   89

Psalm 100:4
THANKSGIVING   *91*

Jewels of Salvation   92
Believer's Benefits   95
Dictionary of Susanisms   97
Index of Scriptures Referenced   99
Notes   102
Bibliography   103

THANK GOD FOR
HIS MIGHTY DEEDS

Give thanks *to the LORD; call upon His name; make known His deeds among the nations. Sing to Him, sing praises to Him; tell of all His wonders. Glory in His holy name; let the hearts of those who seek the LORD rejoice.*

1 Chronicles 16:8-10

This psalm of thanksgiving by David was first sung on the day the Ark of the Covenant was brought back to Jerusalem. God had miraculously returned the Ark to Israel when the Philistine leaders put it on a cart being pulled by two cows who had just given birth to calves. Instead of turning back to take care of their calves, they walked in a straight line to an Israelite town. David's first attempt to move the Ark ended in one man's death because he touched the ark to steady it. David then learned the proper protocol for moving the Ark and made sure all was done according to what Moses had written. There was great relief and rejoicing when the Levites carried the Ark into the tent David had prepared for it. David committed this song to Asaph and his brothers to be sung on this occasion. David began his song of thanksgiving by reminding the Israelites to thank God for his mighty deeds and miracles on their behalf and to spread news of their God to others.

God continues to move in the lives of His chosen people—both Jews and Gentiles who have received Jesus—in unexpected and even miraculous ways. This may seem like an insignificant thing to many, but the Lord placed a seamstress in our path. We hadn't even been praying for one! Since Susan cannot lean forward, all of her blouses must be open in the back to go on like a hospital gown. This sometimes means buying a larger size to accommodate cutting the blouse open and seaming the two edges. Then the shoulder seams droop on her arms. We described that problem to Jennifer at a church craft fair where we both had booths. She believed she could find a solution. She has since modified several blouses and one skirt to fit beautifully. Yesterday, we went shopping with her to purchase material for several skirts with the brilliant idea of having a base skirt with several fronts that could be easily changed without having to roll in the bed. Susan's clothes will now fit perfectly and hang nicely even in her power chair! The Lord literally placed Jennifer in our path! An answer to a prayer we didn't even know to pray!

How has God moved in your life in big or even seemingly insignificant ways? Thank Him and praise Him for His wonderful deeds on behalf of His children. Find something to be thankful for each and every day.

Father, we thank You for sending Jennifer our way. We thank You for providing for our needs. We thank You for all the unseen things You orchestrate in the background that guide our paths in the right direction.

THANKFUL TO BE ENTRUSTED WITH GOD'S RICHES

Both riches and honor come from You, and You are the ruler over all. In Your hands are power and might to exalt and give strength to all. Now therefore, our God, we give You **thanks***, and we praise Your glorious name. But who am I, and who are my people, that we should be able to give as generously as this? For everything comes from You, and from Your own hand we have given to You.*

1 Chronicles 29:12-14

Through Nathan the prophet, God had made clear to David that he would not be the one to build a temple for His Name. Instead, his son Solomon would have that privilege. Therefore, knowing Solomon was young and inexperienced, David began to amass the supplies and money needed for such a momentous endeavor. First, David gave extravagantly of his own treasures. "Then the leaders of the households, the officers of the tribes of Israel, the commanders of thousands and of hundreds, and the officials in charge of the king's work gave willingly" (1 Chronicles 29:6). Read the entire chapter to see how generously the King and his leaders gave to this building fund. David pronounced a blessing on this occasion thanking God for His provision. David had a clear understanding that it was a blessing to be able to contribute and that ultimately everything they had, everything they had given, was given to them by God in the first place.

We feel blessed to be able to give tithes and offerings. Each month, as soon as her SSDI (Social Security Disability Income) posts into her account, Susan has me go to our church website and give her tithe and offering. As soon as I put my checks in the bank, I do the same. We delight to be able to give back to the Lord who so graciously provides for all our needs. When we view everything we "own" as the Lord's and ourselves as stewards of His wealth, it is a blessing to be able to give back through tithes, offerings, or sharing with others in His name.

Have you thanked the Lord recently for the ability to give to Him or to others in His name? Take a moment to think about the ways God has provided for you—income, gifts from others, unexpected blessings of money or goods—and thank Him. Thank Him as you write a check to your church, place money in the offering plate, or give to a fund to help a brother or sister in need. Thank Him for giving you the ability to not only pay your bills but to enjoy giving as well.

Father, we thank You for the way You consistently meet our needs. We thank You for those times we are able to meet a need for a brother or sister in Christ. We thank You for the privilege of giving back to You.

JOYFUL SONG OF THANKSGIVING

*The LORD is my strength and my shield; my heart trusts in Him, and I am helped. Therefore my heart rejoices, and I **give thanks** to Him with my song.*

Psalm 28:7

David had many times when he needed God to be his strength and shield. Enemies pursued him (it seemed regularly) and even his own son Absolom raised an army against him. David always remembered his strength came from God. Even as a boy he slayed the Giant Goliath with God's strength behind the stone as it hurled out of his sling. His confidence was bolstered by the fact that God had already delivered him from wild beasts while tending his father's sheep. "But David said to the Philistine, "You come against me with sword and spear and javelin, but I come against you in the name of the LORD of Hosts, the God of the armies of Israel, whom you have defied" (1 Samuel 17:45). David was God's warrior, but he was also God's singer who glorified the Lord with psalms. God has never had to rescue me (Susie) from wild animals or help me to fight a nine-foot tall giant, but God has been my strength and shield. When my husband left me, I battled a deep depression and even questioned how my loving God could let divorce happen to me. I cried out to the Lord . . . actually, I yelled at Him. He heard my cries and guided me to a singles group who loved me, discipled me, and restored my trust in the God of my salvation. God had to restore not only my trust in Him but my ability to trust and let other people in. The person I had pledged my love to, with whom I had become one flesh, had deserted me. Gradually, that trust in God and His people grew back in me again. As I healed from my hurts, my songs of joy were restored. I once again rejoiced to express gratitude to the Lord with my voice and my piano. Psalm 28:7 became my favorite verse and a memorized reminder in the tough times that the Lord IS my strength and my shield, and I can trust Him.

Are you going through a time when it is difficult to find a reason to give thanks? Make a practice of giving thanks for even the tiniest blessings—a beautiful flower in your garden, a child waving at you in the grocery store, the ability to pay your bills on time. I have found that as I express gratitude to God, He gives me more reasons to be grateful. Think back on previous times you thought you couldn't go on, but God intervened through the thoughtfulness of a friend or the kindness of a stranger. Make thanksgiving a habit, not only a holiday.

Lord, help us to count and be thankful for our blessings rather than wallow in our woes. You are "a shield around me, my glory, and the One who lifts my head" (Psalm 3:3). Increase our faith in You that we may resist being discouraged and drink up the encouragement found in Your word.

MAGNIFY THE LORD WITH THANKSGIVING

I will praise God's name in song and exalt Him with **thanksgiving.**

Psalm 69:30 (BSB)

I will praise the name of God with a song, and will magnify him with **thanksgiving.**

Psalm 69:30 (KJV)

A magnifying glass makes things appear larger than they are. When Susan and I are working together, I temporarily magnify (enlarge) the text to make it easier for her to read on the TV screen. God is already bigger than anything or anyone else. Magnify in this verse means to extol, to exalt, to raise in estimation. In this case, we are magnifying the Lord, extoling His greatness to a world that is too myopic and self-focused to see Him clearly. Notice what magnifies Him: thanksgiving! When we are truly thankful for all God has done and is doing in our lives, and we express that outwardly, we magnify our Lord. Tell people not just that you are thankful, but to whom your thankfulness and praise are directed. Change the phrase "I am thankful" to the more accurate "I thank God." Magnify the Lord God by having an "attitude of gratitude" every day. It will brighten your day and may just give you an opportunity to share the best news ever with someone who desperately needs to hear it! What are some things that can cause us to thank God and share our thankfulness with others?

- I (Susan) thank God that I am breathing. After being placed on ventilator three times in my life, this is a constant praise.
- We thank God for drawing us into relationship with Jesus, Susan at about four years old and Susie at the age of fifteen.
- We thank God for bringing us together that we might each serve Him better.
- We thank God for providing our daily bread (and in Susan's case, the occasional chicken fried steak!)
- We thank God for our church family who have been there for us in so many ways.
- We thank God for the internet which enables us to encourage others even when we are "home-found" most of the time.
- We thank God for our "lifters" who enable Susan to leave the four walls of our room.

We challenge you to make your own list. Thank Him in your private prayers but remember to tell others that you thank God for so much! Be His witness to others by expressing your thankfulness out loud.

Father, as the chorus says, "We've got so much, so much, so much, to be thankful for!"Thank You for the many blessings You bestow on us daily!

*We **thank** You, O True God. Our souls are overflowing with **thanks**! Your name is near; Your people remember and tell of Your marvelous works and wonders.*

Psalm 75:1 (VOICE)

LORD, I THANK YOU

Song lyrics by Susie Hale

Lord, I thank You for the hard times,
for the pain You've brought me through.
Lord, I thank You that the trials
teach me to depend on You.
Lord, I thank You that when I need You,
You are never far away.
Lord, I thank You that You hear me
every time I kneel and pray.

And thank You, Lord, that You loved me
even when I knew You not.
Thank You, Lord, that You showed me
that it was Your love I sought.
When I searched and searched for something
that could make my life worthwhile,
Then You told me You'd adopt me
and that I would be Your child.

And I thank You, Holy Father,
that Your grace extends to me.
Oh I thank You, Precious Jesus,
that You died to set me free.
And I thank You that through Your Spirit,
You can joy and comfort bring.
And I thank You that when I trust You,
You can cause my heart to sing!

THANK GOD FOR HIS OMNIPRESENCE: ALWAYS AVAILABLE

We **give thanks** *to You, O God; we* **give thanks***, for Your Name is near. The people declare Your wondrous works.*

Psalm 75:1

75:1 ***Your name is near.*** God's name represents His presence. The history of God's supernatural interventions on behalf of His people demonstrated that God was personally immanent. But OT saints did not have the fullness from permanent, personal indwelling of the Holy Spirit (cf. John 14:1, 16, 17; 1 Cor. 3:16; 6:19). [1]

One of the attributes of God we are most thankful for is His omnipresence (always being available). Jesus was called Immanuel which means "God with us." When Jesus ascended back to Heaven, He promised a Comforter. That Comforter is the Holy Spirit who is not only with us but IN US! We are NEVER without Him. The Father is only a prayer away, an ongoing two-way conversation. Jesus continually intercedes for us. In the person of the Holy Spirit, the Lord walks with us, guides us, teaches us, and comforts us. The Holy Spirit represents the "alwaysness" of God with His children.

In those times when we feel forsaken by friends, family, or maybe even God, we must remind ourselves that Jesus said, "And surely I am with you always, even to the end of the age" (Matthew 28:20b). When the Holy Spirit came upon the disciples in an upper room at Pentecost, they were filled with God's presence (Acts 2). We as believers are also filled with the Holy Spirit, but sometimes we fail to tap into His power that is available to us 24/7, 365 or 366 in leap years. How do we access the Spirit's power? Remember that two-way conversation? We pray and we listen for and seek God's answer by reading His word.

Do you ever feel alone? Abandoned? Rejected? If you have entrusted your life to Jesus Christ and received His gift of salvation, you will never be alone again. You may FEEL alone at times, but your feelings are deceiving you. Ask the Lord to help you remember and experience His omnipresence. Bring your needs to the Lord with THANKSGIVING, and He will give you peace (Philippians 4:6-7).

Father, constantly remind us of Your omnipresence. Help us to remind each other that "Your name is near" as the Psalmist wrote under Your inspiration.

Worship opportunity and a great chorus to memorize and sing when you feel alone, "No, Never Alone": https://www.youtube.com/watch?v=oUkk7RvctCw

ROCK CONCERT

Come, let us sing for joy to the LORD; let us shout to the Rock of our salvation! Let us enter His presence with **thanksgiving**; *let us make a joyful noise to Him in song.*

Psalm 95:1-2

God, who is the Rock, provided water from the Rock. Numbers 20:8 states, "Take the staff and assemble the congregation. You and your brother Aaron are to speak to the rock while they watch, and it will pour out its water. You will bring out water from the rock and provide drink for the congregation and their livestock." According to 1 Corinthians 10:3-4, Jesus was the Rock that poured out the water, "They all ate the same spiritual food and drank the same spiritual drink; for they drank from the spiritual rock that accompanied them, and that rock was Christ." Jesus, being the Rock, is the provision and is the River of Life. John 7:38 says, "Whoever believes in Me, as the Scripture has said: 'Streams of living water will flow from within him.'" The living water is the Holy Spirit flowing through the life of the believer and bearing witness to the world. The Rock, in scripture, is also a symbol of safety and security. The high rocks of the holy land served as natural fortresses. Jesus is our stronghold, and we rest safely in His care. We thank the Lord that we can continually trust Him and lean on Him. We give thanks for His daily provision, and we thank Him for being our stronghold in times of trouble.

I had only known Susan for eleven months when I stayed in the hospital with her through major surgery. She had come through the bilateral above-the-knee amputation surgery well and was getting settled in a regular hospital room for the night. I had not really eaten since noon, and it was now nearing midnight. While the respiratory therapist was trying to get her oxygen adjusted, I ran down to the cafeteria. I came back to the room, ate two bites of my pizza, and realized Susan's oxygen saturation was too low according to the monitor. The respiratory therapist and the nurse came in to try to replace the nasal cannula with a face mask. I kept telling Susan to breathe. Suddenly the nurse hit a big, red button on the wall and called "Code Blue." Susan had ceased breathing at all! I exclaimed, "Susan, I am not leaving you! I will be in the hallway." She says she was aware of my promise even as they were sitting astraddle her and "bagging" her to squeeze air into her lungs. I sank against the wall in the hallway for fear I would fall, but as I began saying the Lord's prayer (couldn't formulate a prayer of my own at that moment), I realized it was not the wall I was leaning on but the Rock, our Lord Jesus Christ. He faithfully held me up!

Do you remember a time when you had to lean heavily on Christ the solid Rock? Let us sing and shout joyfully to the Rock. Let's hold a "Rock" concert to shout and sing our thanks!

Father, we thank You that we have a solid foundation, a strong Rock, on which to place our faith. Thank You for the many times You have held us up when we thought our knees (or at least Susie's knees since I don't have any) might buckle. May we sing in worship to the Rock of our salvation all our days!

We have sung "Hear My Cry" by Maranatha as our prayer to the Lord many times: https://www.youtube.com/watch?v=Hj4SyA7mpJk

*Come, let us sing for joy to the LORD; let us shout to the Rock of our salvation! Let us enter His presence with **thanksgiving**; let us make a joyful noise to Him in song. For the LORD is a great God, a great King above all gods. In His hand are the depths of the earth, and the mountain peaks belong to Him. The sea is His, for He made it, and His hands formed the dry land. O come, let us worship and bow down; let us kneel before the LORD our Maker. For He is our God, and we are the people of His pasture, the sheep under His care.*

Psalm 95:1-7

I am the good shepherd. The good shepherd lays down His life for the sheep.

John 10:11

I CANNOT HELP BUT SING

I cannot help but sing and shout for joy
to the Rock of my salvation.
I must come before Him with thanksgiving,
singing in exultation:
for He is ruler over everything,
holding the world in His hands.

He made the sea, and from nothingness
spoke into being dry land.
Join me in bowing down to pay homage,
to worship the Lord, our maker.
For we are the flock that He shepherds,
and He is our loving Caretaker.
Come let us sing for joy,
let us shout to the all-powerful King.
Give thanks with me to the Lord, our God,
and thank Him for everything!

CALL UPON HIS NAME WITH THANKSGIVING

*Give **thanks** to the LORD^{H3068}, call upon His name; make known His deeds among the nations. Sing to Him, sing praises to Him; tell of all His wonders. Glory in His holy name; let the hearts of those who seek the LORD rejoice.*

Psalm 105:1-3 (see also 1 Chronicles 16:7-22)

> H3068 - (the) self-Existent or Eternal; Jeho-vah, Jewish national name of God:—Jehovah, the Lord. [2]

Y̵ou may recognize these words from a previous devotional written on the passage in Chronicles, "Thank God for His Mighty Deeds." This time let's focus on the phrase "call upon His name." Exactly what name do we call on? It is the name God revealed to Moses when speaking to him from the burning bush, "I AM WHO I AM. This is what you are to say to the Israelites: 'I AM has sent me to you.'" This is understood to mean that God has always existed and will always exist. He does not really have a past, a present, and a future: He only has always. He is the One who "was and is and is to come" (Revelation 1:4). We have the privilege of taking our needs, our cares, our fears to the Creator of the universe who is omnipresent (always there), omnipotent (all-powerful), omniscient (all-knowing). Once we cast all our cares upon Him (1 Peter 5:7), we need to be careful to express our gratitude to Him for the way He takes care of us. We need to thank God for the joy and the privilege of being His instrument to bless others in His kingdom. When we truly understand whose Name we are crying out to, we cannot help but be thankful that He takes the time not only to hear our cries, but to answer them with action.

Whatever your need is today, you can call upon the mighty name of the Lord. He will answer you in His own way and His own time. Then, thank Him for all He has done, is doing, and will do in Your life. Be sure to also thank the Lord for the many times He has taken care of a need before you even thought to ask Him! "for your Father knows what you need before you ask Him" (Matthew 6:8) and "For the Gentiles of the world strive after all these things, and your Father knows that you need them" (Luke 12:30).

Father, thank You for giving us the privilege to call on Your name in our time of need. Thank You for working mightily for the good of Your children. Thank You for taking even seemingly bad circumstances and using them for our ultimate good and Your glory. We praise Your holy Name!

GRATITUDE FOR GOD'S DELIVERANCE

*Let them **give thanks** to the LORD for His loving devotion and His wonders to the sons of men.*

Psalm 107:8, 15, 21, 31

This Psalm was probably written after the Israelites had been brought back from captivity (see Psalm 107:3). The repeated phrase above urges those who have been delivered to give thanks to the Lord. Several scenarios where thanksgiving is warranted are presented:

- Those wandering in the desert, "For He satisfies the thirsty and fills the hungry with good things" (Psalm 107:9)
- Prisoners in afflictions and chains, "For He has broken down the gates of bronze and cut through the bars of iron" (Psalm 107:16)
- Those who suffered affliction because of sin, "He sent forth His word and healed them; He rescued them from the Pit." (Psalm 107:20)
- Those tossed about in stormy seas, "He calmed the storm to a whisper, and the waves of the sea were hushed" (Psalm 107:29)

Have you ever been thirsty for the Lord? Have you ever felt imprisoned by your past or your sin? Have you ever felt a physical problem was a direct result of disobedience? Have the storms of life tossed you to and fro until you feel battered and beaten? In the scenarios above, the common thread was that these people called upon the name of the Lord, and He heard their cries. You, too, can cry out to Jesus, and He will hear you and deliver you. Then you can join in the chorus of people throughout the ages whom God has delivered by saying "give thanks to the LORD for His loving devotion and His wonders to the sons of men."

Father, we have placed our trust in Jesus, our Deliverer, and give You thanks for Your loving devotion in sending Him to take our place upon the cross, die in our place, and be raised from the dead to ever intercede for us before Your throne. We are grateful for deliverance from sin, from sickness, from cares of this world. We thank You that we are covered by the righteousness of Christ and washed by His blood to stand before Your throne as those who have been redeemed.

Worship our Deliverer and Defender with the song "Trust in Jesus" by Third Day: https://www.youtube.com/watch?v=Hyzb2oM_UPI

THANKSGIVING FOR DELIVERANCE FROM DEATH

*I will offer to You a sacrifice of **thanksgiving** and call on the name of the LORD.*

Psalm 116:17

116:1–19 *See note on Ps. 113:1–9.* This is an intensely personal "thank you" psalm to the Lord for saving the psalmist from death (116:3, 8). The occasion and author remain unknown, although the language used by Jonah in his prayer from the fish's stomach is remarkably similar (Jonah 2:9) While this appears to deal with physical death, the same song could be sung by those who have been saved from spiritual death. [3]

116:17 *the sacrifice of thanksgiving.* Probably not a Mosaic sacrifice, but rather actual praise and thanksgiving rendered from the heart in the spirit of Pss.136 and 138 [4]

The Psalmist was saved from the brink of death when he cried out to the Lord in desperation to deliver him. God has delivered me (Susan) from the brink of death more than once. I was hospitalized due to chronic kidney stones and receiving IV pain medication. The surgeon who had scheduled me for a lithotripsy was not even scheduled to be at the hospital until the next morning. The doctor describes his being there as the Holy Spirit taking his car to the hospital. Since he found himself at the hospital, he dropped by my room to check on me which later became his custom whenever I was hospitalized. He found me unresponsive even after he tried to rouse me a couple of different times. He hit that big red button on the wall to call a code blue resulting in a flurry of activity. I was intubated and remained on vent for three weeks! It was questionable as to whether I would ever be able to breathe on my own again. The pulmonary (lung) specialist even wanted to do a tracheostomy, but my Nana, Mom, and bonus-mom Janelle protested that I was called to preach/teach and would not want to risk loss of my ability to speak. Praise the Lord for my doctor being moved by the Spirit to check on me and obeying that divine direction to drive to the hospital which was not his intended destination! God used him and the medical intervention he initiated to save my life. I have experienced two other times being placed on ventilator since. Therefore, I offer thanksgiving to the Lord for every breath. I sincerely believe the Lord keeps me alive for His purposes. Therefore, I am determined to fulfill my calling to share the good news of Jesus Christ!

Perhaps you are unaware of a time when the Lord saved you from death. However, He may have done so without your knowledge. Perhaps that two-minute delay leaving for work prevented you from being involved in an accident. Maybe God preserved your life in some other way. We should constantly thank the Lord for the gift of life and use the time He has granted us here to share His love with others.

Father, we thank You for intervening on our behalf to preserve our lives. As long as You give us breath in our bodies, we will praise You and tell of Your wonderful deeds.

Thank God by singing "This is the Air I Breathe" by Michael W. Smith https://www.youtube.com/watch?v=mEDcKZB7r2A&t=259s

GRATITUDE TO OUR GOD WHO IS GOOD

Give thanks *to the LORD, for He is good; His loving devotion endures forever.*

Psalm 118:1

"Why do you call Me good?" Jesus replied. "No one is good except God alone.

Luke 18:19

These days, we have watered down the word good. Chocolate is good. Sunshine is good. The pastor is good. My best friend is good. All those things do reflect some aspect of goodness. However, God is the embodiment of every aspect of good: He is consistently and continually well-pleasing, fruitful, morally correct, proper, useful, pleasant, kind, benevolent, abundant, plentiful. God will never fail to be good. The only human that could make the claim of being good was Jesus Christ who knew no sin. In the verse above, He says "No one is good except God alone," however, He never said, "I am not good." In fact, in John 10:30, we read that Jesus asserted, "I and the Father are one." No other human being has the right to say he/she is ALWAYS good. Because of His goodness, God's loving devotion or loving-kindness as the King James Version renders it is everlasting. God does not and *cannot* cease to love His children.

Many times, people question God's goodness and His loving-kindness. "How can a good and loving God let

_____ happen?" You can fill in the blank with the questions you have heard or perhaps even asked. As His created beings, we are incapable of understanding everything He is accomplishing in, through, and for us. However, we can trust His nature and His faithfulness and cling to His promise "that God works all things together for the good of those who love Him, who are called according to His purpose" Romans 8:28. We need to remember that the good He is working is that we become more and more like Jesus, "For those God foreknew, He also predestined to be conformed to the image of His Son, so that He would be the firstborn among many brothers" Romans 8:29. This is why we can thank God for His goodness, kindness, and love even when we do not understand our present circumstances.

We hope you are at a place in your life where it is easy to see the goodness and kindness of our Lord. However, even if you are struggling with the questions that arise during difficult days and have even questioned God's goodness, know that God understands and will never abandon you:

> *Psalm 103:13-14. As a father has compassion on his children, so the LORD has compassion on those who fear Him. For He knows our frame; He is mindful that we are dust.*

Father, we are thankful You are consistently, constantly good, loving, and kind.

Worship with CeCe Winans singing "Goodness of God": https://www.youtube.com/watch?v=y81y-Io1_308&list=RDX9-PxeNrd9c&index=2

*At midnight I rise to give You **thanks** for Your righ-*
teous judgments. I am a friend to all who fear You, and
to those who keep Your precepts. The earth is filled with
Your loving devotion, O LORD; teach me Your statutes.
Psalm 119:62

MIDNIGHT THANKSGIVING

People are in the bars partying at midnight,
offering their praise for the pleasures of this world.
But the psalmist roused himself from sleep at midnight
to offer praise and thanksgiving to his Lord.
He praised the Lord at the darkest hour
Instead of waiting for morning's light.
We need to thank the Lord in our darkest times
While we are still in the midst of a fight.
By faith, we can express thanksgiving
Because our battles are God's, not our own.
We can thank Him in advance for victory
Because we know He is still on the throne.
Jesus is the light of the world,
And His word is a flashlight to guide us.
We need never fear the dark days
With His Holy Spirit inside us.

We can thank the Lord at midnight
As well as the brightness of midday,
For when we call on the name of our Lord,
He will always answer when we pray.

GREAT PRAISE

Give thanks to the LORD, for He is good.
His loving devotion endures forever.
Give thanks to the God of gods.
His loving devotion endures forever.
Give thanks to the Lord of lords.
His loving devotion endures forever.
He alone does great wonders.
His loving devotion endures forever.
By His insight He made the heavens.
His loving devotion endures forever.
He spread out the earth upon the waters.
 His loving devotion endures forever.
He made the great lights—
His loving devotion endures forever.
the sun to rule the day,
His loving devotion endures forever.
the moon and stars to govern the night.
His loving devotion endures forever.
He struck down the firstborn of Egypt
His loving devotion endures forever.
and brought Israel out from among them
His loving devotion endures forever.
with a mighty hand and an outstretched arm.
His loving devotion endures forever.
He divided the Red Sea in two
His loving devotion endures forever.
and led Israel through the midst,
His loving devotion endures forever.

but swept Pharaoh and his army into the Red Sea.
His loving devotion endures forever.
He led His people through the wilderness.
His loving devotion endures forever.
He struck down great kings
His loving devotion endures forever.
and slaughtered mighty kings—
His loving devotion endures forever.
Sihon king of the Amorites
His loving devotion endures forever.
and Og king of Bashan—
His loving devotion endures forever.
and He gave their land as an inheritance,
His loving devotion endures forever.
a heritage to His servant Israel.
His loving devotion endures forever.
He remembered us in our low estate
His loving devotion endures forever.
and freed us from our enemies.
His loving devotion endures forever.
He gives food to every creature.
His loving devotion endures forever.
Give thanks to the God of heaven!
His loving devotion endures forever.
  Psalm 136 (Hallel HaGadol meaning Great Praise)

We have included Psalm 136 in its entirety because the verses containing the words "Give thanks" do not tell us for what the Psalmist was thankful. This psalm would be an antiphonal or responsive reading in which the soloist or priest would make a statement, and the congregation would respond with the refrain "His loving devotion endures forever. "Loving devotion" can also be translated "loving-kindness", "mercy", or in the *Complete Jewish Study Bible*, it is translated "grace". The psalmist was recounting God's faithful care of the nation of Israel.

Challenge: Write your own psalm praising the Lord for specific examples of His loving devotion in your own life. We will share ours with you as the next devotional.

Father, we thank You, the God above all gods, the King above all kings, the Creator of all we know that You extend Your loving-kindness to us daily.

Give thanks as you sing "Forever" with Chris Tomlin: https://www.youtube.com/watch?v=gUH_NzfRmbs

Give thanks *to Adonai, for he is good,*
for his grace continues forever.
Give thanks *to the God of gods,*
for his grace continues forever.
Give thanks to *the Lord of lords,*
for his grace continues forever;

Psalm 136:1-3 (CJB)

OUR GREAT PRAISE

We thank You, God, for our salvation:
Your grace is everlasting.
We thank You we live in a free nation:
Your grace is everlasting.
We thank You Susie became Susan's "Tater":
Your grace is everlasting
We thank You we can learn and work together:
Your grace is everlasting.
We thank You Nana's stroke was mild:
Your grace is everlasting.
We thank You for providing for Susan's care:
Your grace is everlasting.
We thank You for the courage to ask for amputation:
Your grace is everlasting.
We thank You for boldness to share Jesus with hospital staff:
Your grace is everlasting.

We thank You for we are sisters instead of just room-
mates:
Your grace is everlasting.
We thank You for nurse Lindy, LVN Crystal, and PT
Dana:
Your grace is everlasting.
We thank You for the ability to drive a Pink Power Chair:
Your grace is everlasting.
We thank You for disabled vet, Ivan, who drove us to
church:
Your grace is everlasting.
We thank You for Harold helping us to incorporate:
Your grace is everlasting.
We thank You for our bank treating us both as VIPs:
Your grace is everlasting.
We thank You for our van and Eric who found it for us:
Your grace is everlasting.
We thank You for Pastor Ben who encouraged us to pub-
lish: *Your grace is everlasting.*
We thank You for preserving Susan's life in 2019:
Your grace is everlasting.
We thank You for those who helped while Susan was in
ICU: *Your grace is everlasting.*
We thank You for our first book together, *Let Him In*:
Your grace is everlasting.
We thank you Susan was able to attend our first book
launch:
Your grace is everlasting.
We thank you for being able to post Bible studies online:
Your grace is everlasting.

We thank You for Susie's successful spinal surgery:
Your grace is everlasting.
We thank You for a wonderful inpatient rehab for Susie:
Your grace is everlasting.
We thank You Susan could stay at Grandmother's House:
Your grace is everlasting.
We thank You for cash for Susie's surgery and Susan's care:
Your grace is everlasting.
We thank You for transfer teams to lift Susan:
Your grace is everlasting.
We thank You for Dana, Nick S, Nick M, Eric, Zach, Chelsea:
Your grace is everlasting.
We thank You for our Generous Gems—donors to PJM:
Your grace is everlasting.
We thank You for providing for our every need:
Your grace is everlasting.
We thank You for adopting us as Your daughters:
Your grace is everlasting.

THANKFUL WITH ALL MY HEART

*I give You **thanks** with all my heart; before the gods I sing Your praises. I bow down toward Your holy temple and give **thanks** to Your name for Your loving devotion and Your faithfulness; You have exalted Your name and Your word above all else.*

Psalm 138:1-2

Psalm 138:1-2 There is nothing half-hearted about David's thanks. All his powers are employed in blessing Jehovah. And there is nothing timid or private about his worship. He sings unashamedly before the gods, that is, before the kings of the earth. The word "gods" here could also mean angels or idols, but the context seems to limit it to the surrounding rulers.[5]

When David says I will give God thanks "with all my heart," it literally means with every molecule of his being, every ounce of who he is—mind, will, and emotions. How often do we pause to give thanks to God intentionally and intensely? We "ask the blessing" before we eat and thank God for our food. We toss up a thank you when prayer is answered. But do we make time to reflect on our blessings and the way God sustains us and wholeheartedly engage in a prayer of thanksgiving? We challenged ourselves and you to do just that in response to Psalm 136. We wrote "Our Great Praise" yesterday, and the Lord brought much joy to our hearts as we reflected on our journey together as friends who have truly become sisters and as Precious Jewels Ministries, Inc. The personal "psalm" we wrote lists only the highlights of the relationship God has created between us, but counting those blessings and thanking Him for them renewed our resolve to serve Him wholeheartedly.

If you haven't taken the time to write your own "great praise" psalm, please consider doing it. It's a beautiful experience of expressing your gratitude to our loving Creator, Father, Savior, and Lord.

Father, we thank You for inspiring us to write a psalm in the pattern of Psalm 136. Thank You for letting it flow through us with such ease. Remind us to consistently thank You and share with others the marvelous things You have done in our lives.

Enjoy singing "Give Thanks" with CeCe Winans: https://www.youtube.com/watch?v=X9-PxeNrd-9c&list=RDX9-PxeNrd9c&start_radio=1

BE THANKFUL THAT PEACE PREVAILS

On the day I called, You answered me; You emboldened me and strengthened my soul.

Psalm 138:3

Be anxious for nothing, but in everything, by prayer and petition, with **thanksgiving**, *present your requests to God. And the peace of God, which surpasses all understanding, will guard your hearts and your minds in Christ Jesus.*

Philippians 4:6-7

When sores began cropping up on my feet, I did not understand the depth of the problem. They began creeping up my legs despite the doctors' best efforts to cure them and my family's efforts with home remedies. I had only short periods of relief before they returned with a vengeance. I realized the seriousness of the problem when the doctors scraped the wounds to do a culture and nothing definitive came back. They did not have a name for what was causing these necrotic ulcers, so they were unable to come up with an effective treatment plan. I cried out to the Lord for healing, but physical healing did not happen. My feet looked and smelled like they were rotting. One doctor said the danger of sepsis and even dying were possibilities that could occur at any time. The Lord gave me the strength and peace I needed to make the decision to have both legs amputated. On one hand, it was a heart-wrenching decision; but on the other hand, it was a "no-brainer." It was only in Jesus Christ that I could make this choice, and His peace prevailed even during the difficult time of recovery.

Not every time we cry out to the Lord is this drastic (Thank You, Jesus!), but we can be assured that the Lord hears our cry. We can be certain that the Lord is with us; and as long as He is with us, we can have the peace to face any challenge, large or small. He has the power to bring us out of our situation or *through* our situation when we rest in Him as our Prince of Peace. What are you crying out to the Lord about today? Thank Him in advance for the answer and the peace He will provide.

*Father, we can thank You in advance because we know the next time we cry out to You we will experience Your answer to our prayer. We can be at peace because we are confident of Your care. Because we have a relationship with You as our Father, we need **never** walk in worry or fear. Your loving devotion to Your children will **never** fail.*

GIVING FROM GRATITUDE PRODUCES MORE GRATITUDE

You will be enriched in every way to be generous on every occasion, so that through us your giving will pro- duce **thanksgiving** *to God. For this ministry of service is not only supplying the needs of the saints, but is also overflowing in many expressions of* **thanksgiving** *to God.*

2 Corinthians 9:11-12

> **8:1–9:15** This section concerns the collection of money for poor Christians in Jerusalem (cf. Acts 19:21, 22; Rom. 15:25–28; 1 Cor. 16:1–4). [6]

> **8:1–9:15** While this section specifically deals with Paul's instruction to the Corinthians about a particular collection for the saints in Jerusalem, it also provides the richest, most detailed model of Christian giving in the NT. [7]

Generosity is relative. For example, the widow who gave only two small coins but that was all she had (Mark 12:41-42) gave extremely generously. A person who has millions of dollars and gives $1000.00 may not be giving generously or may be very generous depending on his/her other obligations. It's not about the amount. It's about the heart that gives out of gratitude for God's blessings and a desire to minister to those in need. It has been our experience that if God moves us to give an offering above our tithe to a mission trip or a person's medical needs or some other situation, He enables us to give what we have joyfully purposed in our hearts to give. For example, we believed the Holy Spirit was leading us to give toward a mission trip. We were able to put at least $5.00 a week in an envelope toward that gift by giving up our Saturday donuts. We were living on a tight budget at the time but were able to give $100.00. Not much to some people, but it represented a sacrifice of our one budgeted indulgence for several weeks. We were thankful for the opportunity and ability to give, and the minister to whom we gave it was grateful to God as well. I'm sure the people he ministered to gave thanks to God for the mission team's help to them. Grateful giving multiplies the thanksgivings to our Lord.

Is the Lord leading you to give an offering for a specific need? Pray and ask Him to enable you to give generously. We are not to give out of obligation, "Each one should give what he has decided in his heart to give, not out of regret or compulsion. For God loves a cheerful giver" (2 Corinthians 9:7). Giving is an act of expressing gratitude to God for His faithful provision for our daily needs and many unexpected, underserved gifts to us. It is a blessing to give someone else a reason to thank God.

Father, we thank You for providing not just for our needs but enough to share with others. Thank You for the opportunity to pray for others even when we are unable to contribute financially. Thank You for helping us to understand that everything we have comes from You and ultimately belongs to You.

GRATITUDE FOR GOD'S GREATEST GIFT

Thanks *be to God for His indescribable gift!*

2 Corinthians 9:15

9:15 Paul summarized his discourse by comparing the believer's act of giving with what God did in giving Jesus Christ (cf. Rom. 8:32), "His indescribable gift." God buried His Son and reaped a vast harvest of those who put their faith in the resurrected Christ (cf. John 12:24). That makes it possible for believers to joyfully, sacrificially, and abundantly sow and reap. As they give in this manner, they show forth Christ's likeness (cf. John 12:25, 26; Eph. 5:1, 2). [8]

John 12:24 Truly, truly, I tell you, unless a kernel of wheat falls to the ground and dies, it remains only a seed; but if it dies, it bears much fruit.

We have heard the statement that "You can't out-give God" many times and are sure you have, too. God gave His best by sending His only begotten Son to die in our place on the cross. Jesus gave His all—in His humanity, He suffered and died a brutal, torturous death to redeem us and was buried in a borrowed tomb but raised to life on the third day. His death and resurrection began a movement that "turned the world upside down" (Acts 17:6)—Christianity! He had to die in order to redeem those who would believe and cover them with His righteousness, and the result was that His followers multiplied exponentially. After being filled with the Holy Spirit in the upper room, Peter and the disciples preached to the crowds and saw 3,000 people come to faith in Jesus! We, too, have the power to lead people to a saving faith in Jesus, but first we have to die to ourselves in order to live for Christ. "I have been crucified with Christ, and I no longer live, but Christ lives in me. The life I live in the body, I live by faith in the Son of God, who loved me and gave Himself up for me" (Galatians 2:20). Thanks be to God! Jesus is the "gift that keeps on giving." We have the privilege of participating in Christ's ongoing gift by sharing the good news of God's grace with people.

Take a moment to give thanks to God for His indescribable gift—Jesus Christ who died in your place. Ask God to empower you to share this good news with others and thank Him for the honor and privilege of participating in Christ's mission of redemption. Then live each day knowing that you have, "Christ in you, the hope of glory" (Colossians 1:27). Walk in the power of the Holy Spirit and share the gospel in word and deed.

Father, we thank You for Your indescribable gift—Jesus! We cannot completely express in words the mag-

nitude of Your grace, but we are thankful for it! Help us to die to ourselves and live daily empowered by the Holy Spirit to be Your witnesses, sharing the Gospel at every opportunity!

Worship with Phillips, Craig, and Dean singing "Crucified with Christ": https://www.youtube.com/watch?v=_0_1jazh454

GIVE THANKS FOR EVERYTHING

Speak to one another with psalms, hymns, and spiritual songs. Sing and make music in your hearts to the Lord, always **giving thanks** *to God the Father* ***for everything*** *in the name of our Lord Jesus Christ.*

Ephesians 5:19-20

We've heard many sermons or Sunday school lessons on Ephesians 5:18 about not getting drunk but being filled with the Spirit. But we've heard very few indeed on the verses immediately following which define what being filled with the Spirit looks like. As we read over these verses, we couldn't help thinking it would seem a little strange to run around spouting song lyrics at each other. Then I (Susie) took a mental step backward and remembered the importance of music in many of my relationships. I will forever associate "The Band Played On" with the memory of my father taking his little toddler daughter up in his arms and waltzing me around the room while singing that tune. I also hold dear the more recent memory of singing the same song to soothe Daddy to sleep in his hospital room. The lyrics of a song sung by Whitney Houston and CeCe Winans reflect mine and Susan's friendship/sisterhood, "Count on me through thick and thin, A friendship that will never end. When you are weak, I will be strong, helping you to carry on . . ." We count on each other as we count on the Lord together! Song lyrics are powerful. Why shouldn't we encourage one another with Psalms (even more potent because they are God's word), hymns, and Christian song lyrics? Reminding each other of the truths found in them may just help us to obey the next command which is to have music in our hearts directed to our Lord and to be thankful for everything He places in our path. Being filled with the Spirit means we should exhibit the Fruit of the Spirit (Galatians 5:22-23) in our daily lives. Those traits—love, joy, peace, patience, kindness, goodness, faithfulness, gentleness, and self-control—are reflected in many of the lyrics we use to spur each other on as we walk with Jesus. How can we live as conquerors in a world bent on beating us down? Speak courage to each other through the lyrics God has placed in our memories and sing those songs back as praise to the Lord who enabled his servants to write them. Then remember to thank God **for everything**. EVERYTHING? Even the circumstances we perceive as "bad" are used by God for our ultimate good. Faith is standing on that truth even when you don't understand what God is accomplishing.

Not saying you have to belt out a song the next time you greet a friend but do try to encourage others by reminding them of a scripturally sound song. If you put that lyric into their head, they may just walk around singing it throughout the day to be encouraged. If someone is going to have a song stuck in their heads all day, it should be one that encourages them in the Lord!

Father, let the words of our mouths be a witness and an encouragement to others (Psalm 19). Let the songs you have placed in our hearts bring joy and comfort to our family and friends. For you are "my strength and my shield; my heart trusts in you, and I am helped. My heart leaps for joy, and I will give thanks to you in song" (Psalm 28:7 NIV).

"Count on Me" sung by Whitney Houston and CeCe Winans: https://www.youtube.com/watch?v=ae2iX-6vZCoM

BE THANKFUL, NOT ANXIOUS

Be anxious for nothing, but in everything, by prayer and petition, with **thanksgiving**[G2169], *present your requests to God. And the peace of God, which surpasses all understanding, will guard your hearts and your minds in Christ Jesus.*

Philippians 4:6-7

> G2169 *ĕucharistia* – gratitude; act. grateful language (to God, as an act of worship): - thankfulness, (giving of) thanks (-giving). [9]

> G2169 - . . . Eucharist is used in modern language for Holy Communion, embodying the highest act of thanksgiving for the greatest gift received from God, the sacrifice of Jesus. It is the grateful acknowledgement of past mercies. [10]

God's peace will be mounted as a sentinel around our hearts and minds in the midst of situations in which most people would consider it quite normal to be anxious. What is the condition for having that calm, protected feeling? When we begin to worry about something, we must take it to the Lord in prayer with thanksgiving. In other words, we must ask in faith (James 1:6). We need to be able to worship God with gratitude even before the answer to our prayer is visible. We love the definition of faith in Hebrews:

Hebrews 11:1 (AMP) Now faith is the assurance (the confirmation, the title-deed) of the things [we] hope for, being the proof of things [we] do not see and the conviction of their reality – faith perceiving as real fact what is not revealed to the senses.

When we begin to feel anxiety, we need to take the problems that are weighing us down to the Lord and, by faith, thank Him in advance for the peace He will give us. We need to worship Him in our prayers and trust that He only allows those things in our lives that will make us more like Jesus (Romans 8:28-29). Being able to pray with this confidence takes practice. Sometimes our minds must tell our emotions that we are going to trust God whether we feel like it or not. In other words, "Emotions, you are not the boss of us. God is our boss!" We must trust the goodness of God as fact whether our senses or our emotions can see what good can possibly come out of a situation. Fortunately, God understands that we humans struggle with this; and it is okay to pray like the father who brought his son to Jesus for healing, "Lord, I believe. Help thou mine unbelief" (Mark 9:24).

Father, help us to bring all our cares to You trusting that You care for us as your word tells us in 1 Peter 5:7. You are our loving father, and by faith we praise You now for all that You will do in and through us in the future. Thank You for Your loving kindness to us.

Be anxious for nothing, but in everything, by prayer and petition, with **thanksgiving***, present your requests to God. And the peace of God, which surpasses all understanding, will guard your hearts and your minds in Christ Jesus.*

Philippians 4:6-7

Don't fret or worry. Instead of worrying, pray. Let petitions and **praises** *shape your worries into prayers, letting God know your concerns. Before you know it, a sense of God's wholeness, everything coming together for good, will come and settle you down. It's wonderful what happens when Christ displaces worry at the center of your life.*

Philippians 4:6-7 (MSG)

Do not fret or have any anxiety about anything, but in every circumstance and in everything, by prayer and petition (definite requests), with thanksgiving, continue to make your wants known to God. And God's peace [shall be yours, that tranquil state of a soul assured of its salvation through Christ, and so fearing nothing from God and being content with its earthly lot of whatever sort that is, that peace] which transcends all understanding shall garrison and mount guard over your hearts and minds in Christ Jesus.

Philippians 4:6-7 (AMPC)

GIVE THANKS AND LEAVE IT THERE!

We cannot see the answer,
And we struggle, Lord, to trust.
But if we desire to have your peace,
You tell us that we must
Bring everything to You
By petition and by prayer.
Then by an act of faith,
Give thanks and leave it there.

PRAYER OF THANKS FOR BRAND NEW SAINTS

We always **thank** *God, the Father of our Lord Jesus Christ, when we pray for you, because we have heard about your faith in Christ Jesus and your love for all the saints—the faith and love proceeding from the hope stored up for you in heaven, of which you have already heard in the word of truth, the gospel that has come to you. For this reason, since the day we heard about you, we have not stopped praying for you and asking God to fill you with the knowledge of His will in all spiritual wisdom and understanding, so that you may walk in a manner worthy of the Lord and may please Him in every way: bearing fruit in every good work, growing in the knowledge of God, being strengthened with all power according to His glorious might so that you may have full endurance and patience, and joyfully* **giving thanks** *to the Father, who has qualified you to share in the inheritance of the saints in the light.*

Colossians 1:3-6a, 9-12
(see also 1 Corinthians 1:4–9; Philippians 1:3–11)

Some day in the future we hope to write a book on all the prayers of the Apostle Paul, but not today. However, we will state that when Paul prayed for new believers and recently established congregations, he never failed to give thanks to God for their salvation and their growth. We would do well to model our prayers for new believers after the prayers of Paul. Paul not only had a ministry to share the gospel as a missionary/evangelist, but a major part of his work involved encouraging the believers led to the Lord by him or one of his co-laborers. We know this encouragement as the epistles (letters) from Paul to individuals or churches that make up a great portion of our New Testament. Letter writing is almost a lost art in the twenty-first century, being replaced by concise emails and terse texts. We hope our website and printed works serve the purpose of encouraging other believers and possibly leading some seekers to turn to Jesus. In a way, these are letters that reach a broad audience. However, we need to be better about sending a handwritten note or letter when a brother or sister needs a word of encouragement or appreciation.

How long has it been since you received a long letter from a loved one or friend? How long since you wrote one? Perhaps we should all slow down a bit and take the time for letters written on nice stationery. We also need to thank the Lord for new believers and new congregations and pray He will continue to help us invite others into His kingdom.

Lord, we thank You for the privilege of seeing new believers (young and old) grow in their faith. Help us to encourage them and maybe even write them a letter. We thank You for the growth in the knowledge of Jesus, strength, and perseverance we have seen in our own lives and the lives of friends. Show us Your ways and teach us Your paths (Psalm 25:4) then help us to teach others (2 Timothy 2:2).

GOD'S GARDEN OF GLORIOUS, GORGEOUS FLOWERS— PEOPLE OVERFLOWING WITH THANKFULNESS

Therefore, just as you have received Christ Jesus as Lord, continue to walk in Him, rooted and built up in Him, established in the faith as you were taught, and overflowing with **thankfulness**.

Colossians 2:6-7

I (Susie) enjoy growing flowers in the garden and know the importance of the right kind of soil in producing showier flowers. I trim back the roses and crepe myrtles at the right time of year. I get rid of weeds, loosen the dirt, work in peat moss and topsoil, and for some types of flowers add bone meal or plant food. After hours of preparation, I'm ready to plant my annuals. For those flowers to root into the new soil, I keep them properly watered and place them in the proper amount of sunshine.

We are planted into the Lord as soon as we surrender our lives to Him. However, for our roots to grow strong in Him, we need to feed and water them and stay in the light. We feed and water our relationship with Christ by reading His word and listening to godly teachers. We stay in the light by cultivating relationships with other believers and avoiding those situations that plunge us into temptation's darkness.

1 John 1:7 But if we walk in the light as He is in the light, we have fellowship with one another, and the blood of Jesus His Son cleanses us from all sin...

Jesus spoke on the right type of soil in the "Parable of the Sower" (Matthew 13). Be sure you are fertile soil and plant the seeds of the gospel in fertile soil. When plants are planted in good soil, fed, watered, and in proper lighting, they produce magnificent flowers. Flowers seem to glorify God with their entire essence. When we are rooted and grounded in our faith, we do the same thing. The Lord produces a life in us that is overflowing with thankfulness. Giving thanks to the Lord is the equivalent of a rose in full bloom—fantastically beautiful whether it is a large rose or a miniature rose (like Susan LOL) who God literally pruned in 2015 by leading her to have 23 inches amputated from both legs because they were necrotic (dying). We can be God's garden of glorious, gorgeous flowers if we cultivate our relationship with Jesus.

Are you watering the seed the Lord planted in you when He drew you to surrender your life to Jesus? Are you overflowing with thankfulness for His grace and blooming where He has planted you to bring glory to Him?

Father, help our roots grow stronger each day and allow our lives to bloom so that others may see Your glory and glorify You also. Help us to overflow with thankfulness and become like roses in full bloom bringing glory to You, our Gardener.

Worship with the Bill Gaither Trio featuring Susan's first crush (she was 4 at the time) Gary McSpadden singing "Something Beautiful": <u>https://www.youtube.com/watch?v=oj4zC1nIqX0</u>

LET GOD'S PEACE REIGN AND BE THANKFUL

Let the peace of Christ rule in your hearts, for to this you were called as members of one body. And **be thankful**. *Let the word of Christ richly dwell within you as you teach and admonish one another with all wisdom, and as you sing psalms, hymns, and spiritual songs with* **gratitude** *in your hearts to God. And whatever you do, in word or deed, do it all in the name of the Lord Jesus,* **giving thanks** *to God the Father through Him.*

Colossians 3:15-17

God is sovereign—is completely in charge—and when we surrender our all to Him, we will have the peace and confidence to live in harmonious community with our brothers and sisters in Christ. There will be peace in the "familyship" as we each have the peace of submission and obedience ruling in our individual hearts and lives. The word of God is our instruction manual—our life-coach—the source of continuity in living for Jesus. As we fully immerse ourselves, soaking in the Scripture, we will not only have peace ourselves but will be able to encourage others to live and dwell in peace by abiding in the word. As the word begins to seep into and overflow our being, the Lord will infuse us with the power to accomplish all He has called us to do in the grace of and to the glory of God. We need to be steeped in the peace of God. His peace is not a temporary, fragile, worldly peace. It is permanent because He is faithful to His promise,

"Peace I leave with you; My peace I give to you. I do not give to you as the world gives. Do not let your hearts be troubled; do not be afraid" (John 14:27). God's shalom (peace) means that we have wholeness with nothing missing and nothing broken. God's peace should make us into an overflowing reservoir of gratitude and thanksgiving. Although we do not have to earn salvation by good deeds, God has saved us to be "God's workmanship, created in Christ Jesus to do good works, which God prepared in advance as our way of life" (Ephesians 2:10). Therefore, Paul admonishes the Colossians (and us) to do whatever we do "in the name of the Lord Jesus, giving thanks to God the Father through Him."

Do you experience God's peace in your life? Do you go about your work in the name of Jesus and thanking God? Our focus must not be just on the end result of salvation, which is eternity in paradise, but we must have joy in the journey as we experience peace and gratitude. God's peace reigns in our lives and enables us to be thankful as we grow in the grace and knowledge of Jesus. We grow through Bible study, prayer, and fellowship with other believers.

Father, may our hearts burst out in songs of praise and thanksgiving as we realize the peace that passes all understanding has been bountifully accredited to our accounts because Jesus paid the price of our sin on the cross and was raised from the dead. Thank You, Lord, that Your peace permeates our lives in such a way that we need not live in fear and can share peace with others. Help us to continue to trust in Your peace as we grow in our relationship with Jesus.

Let the peace of Christ rule in your hearts, for to this you were called as members of one body. And **be thankful**. *Let the word of Christ richly dwell within you as you teach and admonish one another with all wisdom, and as you sing psalms, hymns, and spiritual songs with* **gratitude** *in your hearts to God. And whatever you do, in word or deed, do it all in the name of the Lord Jesus,* **giving thanks** *to God the Father through Him.*

Colossians 3:15-17

MAY GRATITUDE FLOW

May your peace, Lord, reign in us.
Let your word inhabit our minds.
Allow us to teach with wisdom,
so that others in Your word will find
the peace that they have craved, Lord.
Then with a full heart they may sing.
May gratitude flow from our hearts, Lord,
as an offering of worship we bring.
May whatever we do in word or deed
Be done in the name of Christ Jesus.
May we go through each day thanking You
For His death on the cross that frees us.

May our thankful hearts overflow
As we sing hymns and songs of praise.
May gratitude flow from our hearts, Lord,
As we worship You all our days.

BE VIGILANT AND THANKFUL

Devote yourselves to prayer, being watchful[G1127] *and* **thankfu**l, *as you pray also for us, that God may open to us a door for the word, so that we may proclaim the mystery of Christ, for which I am in chains. Pray that I may declare it clearly, as I should.*

Colossians 4:2-4

> G1127 *grēgŏrĕuō* – to keep awake, i.e. watch (lit. or fig.): - be vigilant, wake, (be) watch (-ful). [11]

> VIG'ILANT, adjective [Latin vigilans.] Watchful; circumspect; attentive to discover and avoid danger, or to provide for safety. [12]

Paul asked the church at Colossae to intercede on his behalf and for his ministry. When I (Susan) was on ventilator due to IV pain meds for chronic kidney stones causing me to become unresponsive and unable to breathe well enough, I had an entire conversation with God in my head. I guess He went to an extreme to keep me from interrupting what He had to say to me. He asked me who did I believe the most underserved part of His body to be. I gave my best guesses—children, the elderly, or the disabled. He said, "No. The most underserved people in the body of Christ are my shepherds and others in ministry." When I was able to speak again, I asked my mom to write down what the Lord had revealed to me so that it would remain clear in my heart and mind. I am thankful the Lord used the horrible experience of being on vent for three weeks to make clear to me what one aspect of my own ministry was to be. For this reason, one stated purpose of Precious Jewels Ministries is to intercede for and encourage other people in ministry. It is our privilege to pray for pastors, missionaries, evangelists, and others who are called to serve the Lord as their vocation. Their job is to equip us for ministry and our job is to intercede for them:

> *Ephesians 4:11-12 And it was He who gave some to be apostles, some to be prophets, some to be evangelists, and some to be pastors and teachers, to equip the saints for works of ministry and to build up the body of Christ.*

You may not be called to full-time vocational ministry yourself. However, you can play a vital role in the ministries of your pastors and other ministers you know (including us). You can intentionally, vigilantly, intercede for them while thanking the Lord for what He has done, is doing, and will do through them and through you.

Father, we thank You for the privilege of prayer. We pray for those who will read this book that You would reveal Yourself to them through answered prayer. Help them find the joy of interceding for others. Help us to continue to be watchful and thankful in prayer.

Devote yourselves to prayer, being watchful and **thankful,** *as you pray also for us, that God may open to us a door for the word, so that we may proclaim the mystery of Christ, for which I am in chains. Pray that I may declare it clearly, as I should.*

Colossians 4:2-4

Pray, and keep praying. Be alert and thankful when you pray. And while you are at it, add us to your prayers. Pray that God would open doors and windows and minds and eyes and hearts for the word so we can go on telling the mystery of the Anointed, for this is exactly why I am currently imprisoned. Pray that I will pro-claim this message clearly and fearlessly as I should.

Colossians 4:2-4 (VOICE)

DILIGENT, VIGILANT PRAYER WITH THANKSGIVING

Lord, help us to be diligent,
devoted to prayer and vigilant
for opportunities to intercede
for brothers and sisters in need.

We approach you with thanksgiving
for the strength for daily living.
We pray for those working to share your word
with people who have never heard.

THANKFULNESS AND JOY
NO MATTER WHAT

Rejoice always and delight in your faith; be unceasing and persistent in prayer; in every situation [no matter what the circumstances] **be thankful** *and continually* **give thanks** *to God; for this is the will of God for you in Christ Jesus.*

1Thessalonians 5:16-18 (AMP)

At this very moment, I am battling sciatic pain, and Susie is battling lethargy due to anemia. We tend to think of thankfulness and rejoicing as feelings, but they are not. They are acts of obedience. We are so thankful that we have learned to be obedient even when we do not understand the reason God is letting us experience trials. We trust that the outcome will be to shape us more into the image of Christ. Our ability to give thanks and be joyful no matter what trial we are experiencing is bound up in our relationship with our heavenly Father. Thankfulness in and for our pain and difficult days is the result of knowing God loves us and chose us when we were unworthy because of sin. We wouldn't even have the capacity to love Him unless He loved us first (1 John 4:19). We can give thanks to God when we pray, even when we are in pain, because He is faithful. We have trusted Jesus, surrendered our lives to Him; and thanksgiving is His will and destiny for us. What the Lord instructs us to do, He empowers us to do through the Holy Spirit within us. This is how we can cry out to God to relieve our pain yet in the same breath thank Him in and for that pain.

Ephesians 5:19-20: Speak to one another with psalms, hymns, and spiritual songs. Sing and make music in your hearts to the Lord, always giving thanks to God the Father for everything in the name of our Lord Jesus Christ.

Do you find it a struggle to obey these verses? Are you in physical or emotional pain that seems too hard to bear? Do you have stress that is weighing you down? Thank the Lord anyway. Thank Him for how He will use those trials to mold you into the image of Christ and thank Him for the way He will answer your cries for help.

Lord, in obedience and by the power of Your Holy Spirit within us, we thank You for the phantom pain, the spasms, the sleep apnea, and all the challenges Cerebral Palsy gives Susan's earth-suit. We thank You for the health problems Susie is battling and for the grace to overcome extreme lethargy to continue to work. We thank You for enabling both of us to continue to minister to others even while experiencing these difficulties. Thank You for giving the calm assurance of joy deep within even during the times of greatest struggle.

Enter His gates with **thanksgiving** *and His courts with praise; give* **thanks** *to Him and bless His name.*

Psalm 100:4

THANKSGIVING

Thoughtful contemplation of all our blessings

Honoring Father God who chose us as His children

Acknowledging that every good and perfect gift
      comes from Him

Nurturing the attitude of gratitude growing within us

Keeping in mind the Lord's forgiveness,
      mercy, and grace

Sacrifice of praise, thanksgiving is an offering
      of ourselves to God

Glorify the One who not sparing His Son,
      sent Him to die for us

Identify Jesus as Father's perfect Lamb
      sacrificed to redeem us

Victoriously extoling the Holy Spirit who transforms us
      from within

Inviting others to join in thanksgiving to God
      for His goodness

Numbering His gifts to us is like numbering the stars:
      impossible

Gladly entering His courts with praise—
              THANKSGIVING!

JEWELS OF SALVATION

❖ *Romans 3:22-24 And this righteousness from God comes through faith in Jesus Christ to all who believe. There is no distinction, **for all have sinned and fall short of the glory of God** and are justified freely by His grace through the redemption that is in Christ Jesus.*

Everyone on earth has sinned. Sin is both doing things that go against what God tells us to do in the Bible and failing to do the good things He instructs us to do. This failure brings the wrath of God on us, and Jesus is the **only way** to make peace with God. John 14:6 "Jesus answered, "I am the way and the truth and the life. No one comes to the Father except through Me."

❖ *Romans 6:20-23 For when you were slaves to sin, you were free of obligation to righteousness. What fruit did you reap at that time from the things of which you are now ashamed? The outcome of those things is death. But now that you have been set free from sin and have become slaves to God, the fruit you reap leads to holiness, and the outcome is eternal life. **For the wages of sin is death, but the gift of God is eternal life in Christ Jesus our Lord.***

The punishment for sin is death. The official term is "substitutionary atonement" which simply means you were sentenced to the death penalty, but Jesus volunteered to die on the cross in your place in order for you to be set free. Jesus died a painful death to redeem you from slavery to sin and spare you from the wrath of the righteous, Holy God.

❖ *Romans 5:6-8 For at just the right time, while we were still powerless, Christ died for the ungodly. Very rarely will anyone die for a righteous man, though for a good man someone might possibly dare to die.* **But God proves His love for us in this: While we were still sinners, Christ died for us.**

Jesus died while we were still sinners. "For God so loved the world that **He gave His one and only Son**, that everyone who believes in Him shall not perish but have eternal life." John 3:16.

❖ *Romans 10:8-10 But what does it say? "The word is near you; it is in your mouth and in your heart," that is, the word of faith we are proclaiming: that* **if you confess with your mouth, "Jesus is Lord," and believe in your heart that God raised Him from the dead, you will be saved.** *For with your heart you believe and are justified, and with your mouth you confess and are saved.*

1 Corinthians 15:3-4 "For what I received I passed on to you as of first importance: that Christ died for our sins according to the Scriptures, that He was buried, that He was raised on the third day according to the Scriptures . . ." If you believe that Jesus is the Son of God who died for you and was raised to life, then trust in, rely on, Him to save you from the wrath of God, you can belong to Jesus.

❖ *Romans 10:11-13 It is just as the Scripture says: "Anyone who believes in Him will never be put to shame." For there is no difference between Jew and Greek: The same Lord is Lord of all, and gives richly to all who call on Him, for,* **"Everyone who calls on the name of the Lord will be saved."**

How do you become a member of the family of God? Pray—talk to God admitting that you cannot be good enough because you could *never* perfectly obey all His commands. Tell Him you trust that Jesus died on the cross to save you from slavery to sin and the wrath of God. Ask God to place His Holy Spirit in you and change you from the inside out. Thank Him for giving you life in His presence forever.

BELIEVER'S BENEFITS

The obvious benefit of trusting in Jesus, the Son of God who died for you and was raised from the grave to return to the right hand of His Father, and surrendering your life to him, is that instead of spending eternity separated from God and all that is good you will live in His presence in complete peace and joy. However, those who become the Lord's children by relying on Jesus gain many other things in this current life on earth. Here are a few:

❖ Lord, we thank you for freeing us from slavery to sin and providing a way to flee temptation! Romans 6:6 "We know that our old self was crucified with Him so that the body of sin might be rendered powerless, that we should no longer be slaves to sin." This does not mean that a believer will never sin again. It means he/she now has a choice to tap into the Holy Spirit's power to resist the urge to give in to temptation. "No temptation has seized you except what is common to man. And God is faithful; He will not let you be tempted beyond what you can bear. But when you are tempted, He will also provide an escape, so that you can stand up under it" (1 Corinthians 10:13).

❖ Lord, thank You that nothing can separate us from Your love! "For I am convinced that neither death nor life, neither angels nor principalities, neither the present nor the future, nor any powers, neither height nor depth, nor anything else in all creation, will be able to separate us from the love of God that is in Christ Jesus our Lord" (Romans 8:38-39).

❖   Lord, thank You that our salvation is secure and cannot be lost! John 10:27-29 "My sheep listen to My voice; I know them, and they follow Me. I give them eternal life, and they will never perish. No one can snatch them out of My hand. My Father who has given them to Me is greater than all. No one can snatch them out of My Father's hand."

❖   Lord thank you for empowering us to do whatever You call us to do! Philippians 4:13 (AMP) "I can do all things [which He has called me to do] through Him who strengthens and empowers me [to fulfill His purpose—I am self-sufficient in Christ's sufficiency; I am ready for anything and equal to anything through Him who infuses me with inner strength and confident peace.]

❖   Lord, thank You for giving us brothers and sisters all over the world! "Respect everyone, and love the family of believers." 1 Peter 2:17a (NLT).

DICTIONARY OF "SUSANISMS"

Bed-found – This is preferred over "bed-bound" because Susan is not chained to her bed, but these days it is usually where Susan is found.

CareGIVER – Caregivers take care of people. Caretakers maintain houses, buildings, or cemeteries! Susie is my caregiver, and I am hers!

Familyship – The family of God. We prefer "familyship" over "fellowship" because, obviously, we are not all fellows.

Framily – Friends who have become family because of our mutual love for Jesus, our brothers and sisters in Christ which may include our biological family as well.

Full-weight - Susan is not "dead weight" when we lift her because she is very much alive! We are simply bearing her full weight because she cannot assist us.

Remnants – Susan does not call her shortened legs "stumps," because stumps are something you put in a woodchipper. Her legs are "remnants" because Jesus saves and returns for the remnant.

Tater – This is Susan's nickname or job description for Susie. It is short for facilitator because Susie facilitates many things for her.

Finally, **PLEASE** do ***not*** refer to Susan as an invalid. She is not IN-valid. Here is her description of herself:

I AM UNIQUELY FIT FOR HIS SERVICE: A DIVINELY DESIGNED PRESENTATION!

INDEX OF SCRIPTURE REFERENCES

Numbers 20:8 — 33

1 Samuel 17:45 — 25

1 Chronicles 16:8-10 — 21

1 Chronicles 16:7-22 — 38

1 Chronicles 29:6 — 23

1 Chronicles 29:12-14 — 23

Psalm 3:3 — 26

Psalm 19 — 67

Psalm 25:4 — 76

Psalm 28:7 — 26, 68

Psalm 69:30 — 27

Psalm 75:1 — 29, 31

Psalm 95:1-2 — 33

Psalm 95:1-7 — 36

Psalm 100:4 — 91

Psalm 103:13-14 — 46

Psalm 105:1-3 — 38

Psalm 107:3 — 40

Psalm 107:8, 15, 21, 31 — 40

Psalm 107:3,9,16,20,29 — 40

Psalm 116:17 — 42

Psalm 118:1 — 45

Psalm 119:62 — 48

Psalm 136 — 50-51

Psalm 136:1-3 — 53

Psalm 138:1-2 — 56

Psalm 138:3 — 58

Matthew 6:8 — 39

Matthew 13   78

Matthew 28:20b   32

Mark 9:24   70

Mark 12:41-42   60

Luke 12:30   39

Luke 18:19   45

John 7:38   33

John 10:11   36

John 10:30   45

John 12:24   63

John 14:27   81

Acts 2   32

Acts 17:6   64

Romans 8:28-29   46, 70

1 Corinthians 1:4–9   74

1 Corinthians 10:3-4   33

2 Corinthians 9:7   61

2 Corinthians 9:11-12   60

2 Corinthians 9:15   63

Galatians 2:20   64

Galatians 5:22-23   67

Ephesians 2:10   81

Ephesians 4:11-12   86

Ephesians 5:18   66

Ephesians 5:19-20   66, 90

Philippians 1:3–11   74

Philippian 4:6-7   32, 58, 69, 72

Colossians 1:3-6a, 9-12   74

Colossians 1:27   64

Colossians 2:6-7   77

Colossians 3:15-17	80, 83
Colossians 4:2-4	85, 88
1 Thessalonians 5:16-18	89
2 Timothy 2:2	76
Hebrews 11:1	70
James 1:6	69
1 Peter 5:7	39, 70
I John 1:7	78
1 John 4:19	89
Revelation 1:4	38

NOTES

1. MacArthur, John, *NKJV MacArthur Study Bible, 2nd Edition,* note on Psalm 75:1.

2. Strong, James, *The New Strong's Exhaustive Concordance of the Bible,* H3068.

3. MacArthur, note on Psalm 116:1-19.

4. MacArthur, note on Psalm 116:17.

5. MacDonald, William, *Believer's Bible Commentary,* note on Psalm 138:1-2.

6. Sproul, R. C. *ESV Reformation Study Bible,* note on 2 Corinthians 8:1-9:15.

7. MacArthur, note on 2 Corinthians 8:1-9:15.

8. MacArthur, note on 2 Corinthians 9:15.

9. Strong, G2169.

10. Zodhiates, Spiros, ed., *The Complete Word Study Dictionary: New Testament*, G2169.

11. *Strong*, G1127

12. Webster, Noah, *The American Dictionary of the English Language, 1828*, definition of "vigilant".

BIBLIOGRAPHY

MacDonald, William, *Believer's Bible Commentary,* (Thomas Nelson, 2016).

MacArthur, John, *NKJV MacArthur Study Bible, 2nd Edition,* (Thomas Nelson, 1997, 2006, 2019), as quoted on www.biblegateway.com

Rubin, Rabbi Barry, *The Complete Jewish Study Bible,* (Hendrickson Publishers, 2016).

Sproul, R. C. *ESV Reformation Study Bible*, (Reformation Trust Publishing of Ligonier Ministries, 2021).

Strong, James, *The New Strong's Exhaustive Concordance of the Bible,* (Thomas Nelson, 2009).

Webster, Noah, *The American Dictionary of the English Language, 1828.* as found at https://webstersdictionary1828.com/

Zodhiates, Spiros, ed., *The Complete Word Study Dictionary: New Testament* (Chattanooga, TN: AMG Publishers, 2000).

ABOUT THE AUTHORS

SUSAN SLADE is an ordained minister (Fellowship of Churches and Christian Ministries, now a part of Kerygma Ventures). She earned a BA in English Bible with minors in Pastoral Counseling and Modern Hebrew and a MA in Biblical Literature from Oral Roberts University in Tulsa, Oklahoma. She is the founder and president of Precious Jewels Ministries, Inc., a 501(c)3. She was a guest of "Life Today" with James Robinson. The Lord enables Susan to overcome Cerebral Palsy to serve Him with joy. She previously wrote a devotional book titled A Life's Symphony of Joy and co-authored a year-long devotional titled Let Him In and two shorter books titled Thirty Days of Thanksgiving Praise, and From Prophecy to Perfection: A Treasury of Christmas Devotions with her partner in ministry Susie Hale.

KAREN SUE HALE (SUSIE) has a BA in Music Education and a M.Ed. with a focus on language arts and serves as Vice President and Secretary of Precious Jewels Ministries. In addition to co-authoring books with Susan, she previously had two articles published in "Purposeful Singleness Monthly" and one published on "Christian Women Today," a webzine. Susie taught eleven years at Glenview Christian School in Ft. Worth, Texas and served as curriculum coordinator there. Susie is Susan's "facilitator" assisting with daily living and more importantly Bible study, making use of her language and computer skills.

ABOUT PRECIOUS JEWELS MINISTRIES

The mission of Precious Jewels Ministries is to inspire, educate, encourage, and console the body of Christ and to present the gospel of grace to a lost and dying world. The goal is to minister to pastors, laypersons, and new believers through verse-by-verse Bible studies, articles, devotionals, speaking engagements, intercessory prayer, and scriptural blessings. Check out the resources available, order more books, and read devotionals online at: **https://www.preciousjewelsministries.com**